FURST

Soft suede, supple leather

Soft Suede,

Supple Leather

CRAFT AND DESIGN

RONALD KENNETH FURST

SIMON AND SCHUSTER | NEW YORK

Thank you

The staff and my students at the Craft Students League in
N.Y.C.; Janis Savitt, Raphael Macia, Lisa Maria Kearing, Anita
Linda Furst, Peter Polymenakos, Kathleen Collins and Felix,
and Julie Houston; and to the people who reluctantly stood
before the camera, Howard Chapman, Daryl, Despina Greco,
Phyllis Krim, Barbara Washburn, Lauren Walker, Ramol Sher-
man. Also Jack Cronin and Sy Rubin.

SBN 671–21706–2
Library of Congress Catalog Card Number: 73–18112
Manufactured in the United States of America
1 2 3 4 5 6 7 8 9 10

CONTENTS

FOREWORD

For nearly four years, I designed, manufactured and sold handmade leather goods for my own and other boutiques. During that time people often asked me to teach them the craft simply for their own enjoyment. In the fall of 1971, the Craft Students League in New York met the growing demand for new courses in leatherwork and formed a Creative Leather course. I was asked to teach that course. My students frequently asked why there were no books that gave simple instructions for original, tasteful leather designs, and that is how I came to write this one.

There are only a few easily available tools needed; a kitchen table or a desk makes an ideal workshop. You will learn all the simple basic methods involved and how to apply them to the creations that I have presented in these pages. You will not have to invest a large amount of time and money, and with a bit of practice you can make some great things.

Leather as a craftsman's material has what can be described as a sensuous feeling. It also has unlimited potential for craft and design.

I have purposely chosen basic, useful and popular designs to illustrate a range of leatherwork techniques. For those who have worked with leather, I hope some of the ideas shown here will encourage you to design and produce your own creations, just as I hope newcomers will find the means to make this a satisfying new hobby.

R. K. FURST
New York City
July 1973

1. A mural of Thothmes IV, from his tomb in the Nile Valley, depicts the king hunting in his chariot. On his left forearm is a wristguard of leather which protects him from the bowstring. Two leather quivers are strapped diagonally across his shoulders, another leather quiver and bowcase are fastened to the side of the chariot. The horses' bridles and reins, the "tires" and the decorated sides of the chariot are also made of leather.

I

Timeless Leather
—A Brief History

Since man's civilized beginnings he has been aware that leather is a most useful material.

The first humans probably did not attempt to provide themselves with clothing until they migrated to the colder northern regions. Man's first wardrobe consisted of leaves and wild grass; the hides of animals followed. About 30,000 years ago, Cro-Magnon man gained for himself the knowledge that the hide of dead animals was splendid for keeping himself warm. After being scraped with stone and washed, the hides were dried. The then hard and brittle skin was hung around the wearer's neck or waist and held in place by either a thorn or a strip of the skin. Natural oils from the man's body rubbed off on the skin, producing the first crude tanning.

Leather has been in widespread use for garments and home furnishings since 3000 B.C. by the very crafty Egyptians. The oldest actual leather ever found was in the form of a pair of sandals, discovered on an archaeological expedition to Sakkara, in Egypt. The Egyptians learned that leather was an excellent material for use in battle. It was employed for tent shelters and weapon carriers as well as for body covering. Warrior Pharaohs found ox hide to be very tough and durable, and its strength and thickness made it

superb for armor. The ox skins were soaked in a hardening solution diluted with water and then pounded on wooden forms in the shape of the human chest. Leather was also used to cover the wheels of chariots.

The Egyptians also produced high-quality furniture with leather. Chairs and divans were constructed with webbed leather strips that were knotted and mounted onto carved wooden frames. Furniture of this fashion is as comfortable and stylish as anything manufactured today.

Four thousand years ago, Egyptian women prized leather for fashion in much the same way as women do today. Trading parties found the hunters of the Nile valley willing to trade their panther and leopard hides for beads and fabrics. Small barges transported the skins hundreds of miles up-river to the waiting designers of the Egyptian fashion world. Communication across the entire African continent was made possible by the use of large drums. The drums were made from large hollowed-out logs with an animal skin, usually cowhide, stretched tautly over the top.

The Egyptians were the greatest tanners in history. They perfected the art of mummification and probably applied this knowledge to the preserving of animal skins. Their mummies, as well as some examples of leather-

2. My copy of an Egyptian mural (circa 800 B.C.) depicting sandal making, from a tomb at Beni Hassan. Right to left: softening the skin; piercing the pattern with a copper awl; shaping the sandal; adding the straps.

work, have survived 5000 years. In ancient Greece and Rome tanners discovered the preservative qualities of the leaves and bark of certain trees—such as the elm—and produced leather by soaking animal hides in a solution of herbal juices mixed with water. Goatskins were used to make maps. And almost the same kind of cowhide sandals designed and made around 200 B.C. are being copied today by some craftsmen.

During medieval times the art and industry of tanning leather flourished in the Near East. Many kinds of leathers were introduced to Europe by the Moors. When caravans of traders crossed the desert on camels they carried hand-painted and hand-stitched pigskins filled with drinking water. These oil-tanned pigskins were completely waterproof.

Arabs settling in Spain introduced decorated leather to the region. The wall hangings of Cordova enjoyed international renown. In the 15th century, Spanish leather was used to cover walls and floors and to upholster armchairs and sofas.

In England, in the 16th century, leather entered a romantic period during the time of Elizabeth I and Shakespeare. The legendary Robin Hood wore a high-peaked, soft leather hat and leather tunics sometimes decorated with nailheads. In the pubs of England, men drank their ale out of leather mugs that they usually had made themselves.

Toward the 17th century, Holland, France and Italy (the artistically progressive cities of Florence and Venice in particular) began competing with Spain to capture the interior design market. Wallpaper, though fashionable, was not accepted by the Dutch. Instead, they instructed workmen to install embossed leather as wall covering. The results were quite beautiful, but as the 18th century neared, the wallpaper industry nevertheless had eliminated most leatherwork on walls.

During this time, the fashion rage of the French nobility was high-cuffed leather gloves. Tanning processes had been perfected as far as curing and preserving were concerned, but a most disagreeable odor resulted. The French found this absolutely intolerable, so the gloves were bathed in perfume by the tanners. As all the tanneries were located in the south, largely at Grasse, the perfumers all flocked to this district to sell their products. Years later the tanneries were moved to different locations but the perfumers stayed in the south of France, thus creating the world-famous region where French perfume as we know it today is produced.

In November of 1519, Hernando Cortes, the Spanish adventurer, landed in Mexico. There he found Montezuma and the Aztecs quite knowledgeable in the art of working in leather. But the Spanish invader was not as interested in the lovely leatherwork itself as he was in the

3. *An outstanding example of 18th-century Spanish leatherwork. This is a section of a tooled and carved wall hanging. The flowers and birds were given greater emphasis by impressing the background with a triangular stamp. The flowing and swirling figures are produced with remarkable skill.*

gold used for its embossing. Cortes destroyed the entire nation in order to get this gold.

For the North American Plains Indians, leather was essential for survival. Their homes were tepees, lightweight leather tents that could be dismantled and transported when the tribe was following the buffalo herds. In winter the skins of buffalo kept the lodgings warm and were used to make thick cape-coats for both men and women. These were worn with the fur side in and the men would paint scenes of themselves in battle on the smooth side. In summer, soft deerskins were used to make decorative clothes for the entire tribe. Beaded leather moccasins were worn and all the great warriors had fantastic clothes decorated with beads or fringe, bone or porcupine quills. Sometimes the Indians would ask European designers to make leather clothes for them. The hunters of the great Sioux nation would disguise themselves under beaver skins in order to fool the buffalo. They would crawl to within bowshot distance of their prey and then strike. The white man out west used leather for saddles and chaps, holsters and harnesses, as well as for clothes.

Victorian England and the rest of Europe were at the time obsessed with ornamentation unrelated to any practical function. Leather trunks for traveling were made weighing from 50 to 100 pounds. A woman then traveled with 10 to 20 hats at least, in hat boxes that weighed over 20 pounds. Porters, however, had not yet been unionized.

The interior designers of the 1920's and 1930's, notably the Bauhaus people, rediscovered the supple luxuriousness of sleek and overstuffed leather chairs and sofas. Designers such as Le Corbusier and Marcel Breuer used large cowhides to make rectangular pillows and usually complemented them with a frame of polished steel. Book binders had a bit of fun with all

4. This 1861 painting by George Catlin shows the extensive use of leather by the Indians. Black Rock, the war chief of the Sioux tribe, is wearing a magnificent outfit. His cape is a buffalo skin decorated with stylized paintings and pictographs of the chief in victorious battle. The young woman on the left wears a buckskin dress with buffalo cape. The chief's wife, on the right, carries a cradle of decorated leather which is held on her head with a band of leather. She, too, is wearing a fringed, decorated dress. All three are wearing leggings and moccasins of buckskin. The small child on the right is undoubtedly freezing and asking his mother for something to wear.

5. *Fine bookbinding, like this 1929 French example, can be an art. The rhythmic flow of the design makes the cover as attractive as the text. The goat-skin is brown with contrasting areas of beige and black. The meander pattern is stamped in gold and silver. The endleaves are brown suede.*

the incredible Art Deco patterns and print types that were popular at the time.

The walls of luxury cruise ships were decorated with leather. The *Normandie*, for example, even had leather-upholstered chairs and lounges, matching the walls. Leather was used for car interiors and a few frivolous Europeans were seen with roadsters with patchwork suede seats.

At one time or another throughout history leather has been used for every known item of human attire. Most of these items are still being made. Hats, coats, dresses, shirts, skirts, and trousers; gloves, bags and wallets, boots and shoes, sporting equipment, industrial products, and furniture are all being made from leather. Many people today are enjoying the natural-ness of working with leather. Technology eases our lives and provides more leisure time for work with our hands. It also creates a need to return to more natural, simpler ways.

2

All About
Skins and Leather

Leather is an animal skin that has been converted by chemical or other processes—known as tanning—into a useful condition. Tanning preserves the skin, and protects it against extremes of temperature and humidity. Many kinds of leather will remain undamaged even by boiling water. Tanning can make the skin soft and resilient, flexible but strong, and able to withstand considerable abrasion. It is an excellent design material: it resists tears and punctures; it can be either somewhat elastic or stretch-resistant, depending on the way it is tanned; it can be refinished to achieve a new effect; it can keep one cool in summer or warm in winter because of its ability to "breathe."

The process of how an animal skin becomes a usable piece of leather actually begins with the birth of the animal itself. The kind of life the animal leads will have a direct influence on the final look of the skin. If the animal has had a comfortable and sheltered life the skin will be smooth; if it has had a hard life, the scars and marks of its existence will show, even after tanning. Whether it is cowhide, goatskin, sheep, rabbit, elephant, snake, kangaroo or even shark, no two skins will ever be exactly alike—the color, grain and texture vary according to the whim of nature.

The tanning process consists of several stages. A hide has to be preserved immediately or it will begin to decompose. This is done either by dry salting (placing salt on the moist hide and then totally drying it out) or by wet salting (placing salt on the hide, letting it dissolve in the natural moisture of the hide and keeping it wet). In their preserved state, the skins are then washed in huge revolving drums. This removes all water-soluble materials from the skins.

The next step is called fleshing. This is done with a machine that scrapes off all flesh and fat on the inside of the hide itself. If need be, this process could be performed with a knife as the Indians might have done it. Removing the hair follicles is the next step. Modern technique calls for the skins to be washed in a solution of lime. This dissolves the hair follicles. Ancient methods would call for hand scraping with a knife to perform this task.

There are different tanning solutions and the ultimate use of a skin determines which solution will be used. For example, tanning cowhides with oil produces supple skins that are used for garments. Indian women took the brain, fat and milk of a buffalo, mixed them together, and scrubbed the mixture into the hides. The skin would then be washed and scrubbed again. This method produces a very soft leather. By tanning their animal skins by hand, the Indians produced the finest leather in the world.

Suede is made by taking a cowhide and placing it under a large revolving cylinder covered with an abrasive similar to sandpaper.

Most leathers will vary in thickness. A leather splitting machine actually takes the skin and splits it into different layers, each meant for a special purpose. A suede split is the underside layer of a cowhide. Patent leather is produced by continuous spray-painting and drying and repainting the skin with a flexible enamel paint.

Chrome tanning is the most widely used method for tanning today. This is done by soaking the skin (after fleshing, dehairing and resoaking with acids to remove all the chemicals) in a drum filled with chromium salts. Vegetable tanning means processing leather in vegetable material derived from the bark and wood of trees. Tanning with certain types of fish oil or codliver oil produces very soft leathers such as chamois. Once it has become leather, the skin can receive some color. The leather is dyed either by placing it in a revolving drum containing liquid dye or by stretching the skin on a frame and spray-painting it.

Buying Leather

When you are in a leather store or a hobby shop and are about to purchase your skins, ask if you can lay them out on a table for inspection. No two skins are ever going to be exactly alike. Some skins may have distinguishing scar marks—which may or may not add to the character of the skin. For the most part, look for skins which have no scars, or which bear scars only at the edges. Some leather may also have holes in the center of the skin. These skins should be avoided if possible, especially if you are working with large patterns for bags or garments. When working with patterns for small or long thin items, however, it is usually possible to work around the holes.

If you are buying suede, run the palm of your hand over the skin and then look at your hand. If it is covered with a thin layer of "suede dust" (which is actually the dye), don't buy the skin. This dust usually doesn't stop rubbing off on clothes for weeks. On certain high-quality sueded leathers the test will result in a small amount of the dye rubbing off. This "crocking," as it is called, will usually cease in a day or two. Suede splits, which average in size from about 5 to 10 square feet, come in a wide variety of colors. The colors of all leather vary according to the season. In fall and winter, the more subdued blues, browns and greens are sold. In spring and summer the bright reds, yellows and pastel colors will be found in the stores.

Buying leather is different from buying fabric. When purchasing fabric, you simply pay by the yard. Because of their irregular character, leather skins are sold by the square foot. There will be two digits somewhere near the edge of every skin. The skins might be numbered thus: 62, 51, 73, or 81. The first digit—6, 5, 7, 8—refers to the square footage of the skin. The second digit—2, 1, 3, 1—refers to the fraction of remaining footage on any one skin. The second digit will always be a 1, 2, or 3. This means one-third, one-half, or three-quarters of a foot. Therefore, 62 means 6½ sq. ft., 73 would indicate 7¾ sq. ft., and 51 would be 5¼ sq. ft. A single digit on the skin means that there is no extra fraction and that the footage is exact.

When making a garment, you must be sure to buy the exact amount of leather footage for your pattern. Ideally, you should buy leather in person and lay your pattern pieces down on the hides when you are actually in the store. If you are ordering leather, I suggest sending a copy of your pattern (a newspaper duplicate will do) to the mail order supply house.

Leather Weights

The weight of leather is determined by the number of ounces that one square foot weighs. For example: If a square foot of leather weighs eight ounces it is called 8-ounce leather. It would also be approximately one-eighth of an inch thick. Most garment leathers will be two-and-a-half or three-and-a-half ounces per foot.

The chart below shows the approximate bulk of the leather appropriate for various articles in ounces per square foot.

1 2 3 4 5 6 7 8 9

6. *The thickness of leather in ounces per square foot*

PROJECT	LEATHER (BULK) REQUIRED (IN OUNCES)
Belts with lining	3–6
Belts, unlined	6–10
Handbags	3–5
Attaché Cases	4–6
Cushions/Pillows	4–6
Garments	2–3
Watchbands	4–6
Linings for bags	1–2
Furniture (unsupported)	8–10

If possible, try to purchase leather from a wholesaler or manufacturer in your own city or town. Look in the yellow pages or business telephone directory under leather or hides or skins. A call to your local Chamber of Commerce might be helpful. Some companies will not sell leather in small quantities; a phone call will determine this.

In the back of this book there is a listing of some establishments across the country that sell leather. Some of these will accept small mail orders. If purchasing skins is not possible on a wholesale or other less expensive basis, you will have to buy them at a local hobby shop or department store. Some fabric and notion stores are beginning to stock leather.

I have found that the best all-purpose leather is garment cowhide sides. This strong, supple leather is reversible. One side is leather and the other side is suede. These skins may be anywhere from 12 to 20 square feet. This leather is ideal for making laces. As the name implies, garment cowhide is used for making clothes. It comes in many different colors. Anything made from this leather takes on a darker, shiny surface within a few weeks. This adds greatly to the looks of the article.

Kinds of Leather

Illustration 7 shows the parts of a skin. The most useful portion of the leather is the back. The weakest section of the skin and the part most susceptible to stretching is the belly.

LATIGO COWHIDE is a heavy leather that comes in only one color—natural—but it can be dyed if you wish. It is used for the backing of belts, where sturdiness is required, and also for bags and attaché cases.

7. A: The back or center of the skin is the strongest part and has the least tendency to stretch.

   B: Scars may be found on either side of the skin and should be avoided if possible.

   C: Holes are easy to spot and should be avoided.

   D: The belly is the weakest portion of the skin and has the greatest tendency to stretch.

   E: The skin might be cut up as indicated by dotted lines and sold as sides.

   F: The shoulder may be wrinkled; it might be used for making laces.

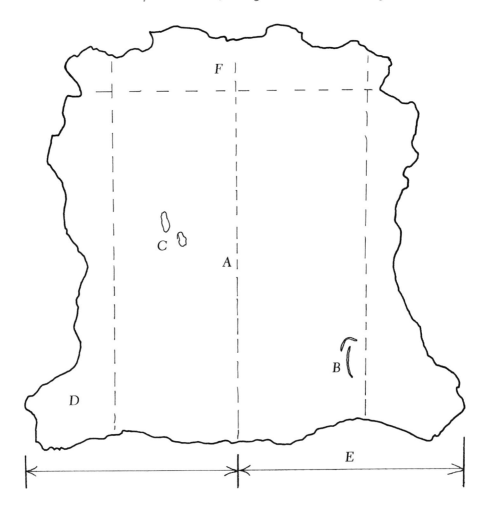

ANTELOPE. A soft leather with velvety nap, used for the finest gloves and handbags.

BUCKSKIN. A sueded leather made originally from deerskin. It is tanned with fish oil or formaldehyde. Good for a variety of uses.

CALFSKIN. A small skin used for small items and for trim on garments.

CABRETTA. The word is from Spanish for goat, but actually the leather comes from a special sheep. Cabretta may be used for clothes and bags but it is thin and has a tendency to stretch. This problem can be overcome by attaching a thin lining.

CHAMOIS. A soft-sueded leather originally made from the skin of the antelope but now made from sheep- or lambskin tanned with fish oil or codliver oil. The skins are small but can be pieced together to make garments. This is a very fashionable leather at the moment. It is soft against the body and it is washable.

CROCODILE. Crocodile (or alligator as it is called in the United States) is a very attractive, scaly leather. The skin comes with its own natural enamel and patterns. The back of the crocodile is much too coarse to use for leather. Only the belly, which is the weakest part, can be used. It is usually used for very expensive bags and wallets. Because of fear of extinction of the species the sale of crocodile leather has been outlawed in some states.

DOESKIN. A soft, supple leather with a fine suede finish. Now this leather for garments is made from lamb- or sheepskin.

Frog. Japanese frog skins, when they can be obtained, make fine wallets. Their small size limits their use.

Lizard. Indian lizard skins come in many colors and have tiny scales.

Cobra. Small snakeskins dyed different colors and used for trim on some leather items. Recently some cobblers in England have begun making shoes and boots of cobra.

Ostrich. A leather distinguished by small bumps left on the skin of the bird after the feathers have been removed.

Pigskin. The vegetable-tanned skin of a pig. This firm waterproof leather is ideal for garments needed in rough weather. Pigskin is used to make sporting equipment. It also has very little tendency to stretch. Little holes grouped in threes, left from the removal of the hair, characterize this leather.

Sealskin. Black shiny leather with excellent wearing qualities.

Sharkskin. Usually brown and white or black and white, this skin is characterized by very small scales. Sharkskin is a novelty leather that sometimes is used for shoes and boots.

Python. A rather large snakeskin, dyed various colors and used for boots and shoes. In Africa, very attractive bags are made from python skins.

Elephant. A very tough gray or brown leather, most suitable for shoes and luggage, said to be virtually indestructible.

Rabbit. A small, furry skin used for coats and hats and for trimming garments.

Sheepskin. Comes in three thicknesses: one quarter inch, one half inch and one inch. This leather is great for making a warm coat. The sueded outside may be dyed or left to weather naturally.

Size and Weight of Commonly Used Skins

LEATHER	SKIN SIZE (BY SQUARE FOOT)	WEIGHT (BY OUNCES PER SQUARE FOOT)
antelope	5–9	2–3
buckskin	5–9	2–4
chamois	5–8	2–3
sheepskin	7–9	2–3, 3–4, or 4–5
garment cowhide	20–40	2–3
calfskin	5–9	2–3
pigskin	5–8	2–3
latigo cowhide	15–25	3–10
suede split	5–9	2–3
kidskin	3–6	1–2
python	8–20	1

Sometimes a pile of first-grade leather skins will be grouped together and sold at a lower price because of numerous scars or holes. If you are working with small projects try to locate such bargains. And if you are buying in quantity, ask for a discount. You might obtain one ranging from 5 to 20 percent.

3

Your Workshop and Tools

Some people think that to work in leather requires an elaborate workshop and huge expenditures for equipment. This is not true at all. For years I did all my work right on my dining table, and you can do the same. Any large table or flat-topped desk will make an ideal workshop. If you use either one, cover it with a sheet of metal or a piece of plywood or pine to protect the surface. A waste basket should be kept handy to hold all the minute scraps (such as hole punchings) as they accumulate.

Store your tools near your work area. A pegboard with hooks, or a handmade leather bag or old cardboard box can hold tools and supplies. Small plastic containers or jars will serve to hold small rivets, eyelets and snaps. These items tend to get mixed up or stepped on, and are a nuisance if not properly stored.

Leather skins should be rolled up and kept in a box. Do not cover the skins with plastic; paper is better. If you are working with any kind of dye, exercise extreme caution. Bottles of dye should be kept tightly closed when stored—and don't keep the tops off when using them. Store the dyes with paints and cleaning fluids as a reminder of their power of destruction. When dyeing, spread a generous supply of newspaper underneath, above, below—everywhere the dye might accidentally touch.

Lighting

Light your work area well with either an area light or good general illumination. Cutting leather requires extremely good light, otherwise it is difficult to follow the guidelines drawn on the leather. A small, high-intensity lamp is good for concentrated lighting when needed. I have often enjoyed working on a bare floor with natural sunlight as my lighting.

Inspiration for projects can be provided by photos or drawings of interesting designs you've seen in leather. Tape these to a wall or put them in a notebook to remind yourself of something you would like to make.

A comfortable flexible desk chair is the best type of seating. An old office chair recovered in suede would be ideal.

Necessary Tools

The cost for all the tools needed for the projects in this book might come to a grand total of about $20.00. Here is a list of tools and supplies to buy and some suggestions on where to obtain them.

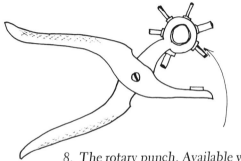

8. The rotary punch. Available with changeable dies.

SIX-HOLE ROTARY PUNCH is the most important tool you will be using. The punch is shaped like a pliers but has a rotating head consisting of six different punch sizes. The smallest is number 1, the largest is number 6. Some punches are obtainable with screw mounts for replacing the little punches that wear out after a year or two of regular use. Most hobby stores carry the rotary punch. Buy a good one and stay away from the one-dollar special.

9. Drive punch

DRIVE PUNCH makes holes in places the rotary punch will not reach. This tool is also handy when your hand hurts from squeezing all those holes with the rotary. Actually, you will gradually build up strength in your hand and overcome this problem. The drive punch is about five inches long with a hollow bottom and comes in some six different hole sizes. These correspond approximately to the sizes on the rotary punch. When working with the drive punch it is necessary to place a small piece of wood or masonite under the work. Place the punch over the work and hit it with the hammer. The wood underneath prevents any damage to the table and to the punch-cutting edge. These punches are available from the Tandy leather stores across the country, as well as in some hardware stores.

10. Awl

AWL has a short wooden handle with a 3″ or 4″ metal point. This tool, which is similar to an ice pick, has two functions: it widens the

11. Shears. Overall length between 7″ and 10″.

holes through which laces pass and it makes holes for sewing with a needle and thread. An awl will be found in any hobby, leathercraft or hardware store.

SHEARS are necessary for most of the cutting of leather and lacing. The important thing to remember is that the shears are going to be in your hand a considerable amount of time, so be sure to find a pair that feels comfortable. The average shears should be no longer than 10″ and no shorter than 7″ in overall length. Sharp tailor's shears are effective for cutting leather. Left-handed craft workers should remember to buy only left-handed shears; there is a great difference in the shaping of the handle. Some shears cut more smoothly than others, so it is a good idea to take along a small piece of scrap leather and test the shears before buying. Shears should cut easily and not "pull" the leather. If you are going to undertake a project using heavy latigo cowhide, a razor knife ("handyman" knife) will be required. This tool can be obtained in any art, hardware or hobby store.

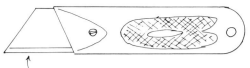

12. "Handyman" knife with changeable blades.

HAMMER. I am about to break with a long-standing tradition among leathercrafters and say that you do not need either a rawhide or a wooden mallet. An ordinary hammer (usually from the nearest toolbox) used gently will do just fine.

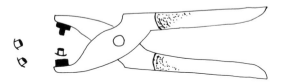

13. *Eyelet setter and eyelets*

EYELET SETTER is used for setting eyelets in belts or where needed. Occasionally different colored eyelets can be found. An eyelet setter and a supply of eyelets can be obtained at the notions counter of most department stores and possibly at five-and-dime stores or at hobby shops.

GLUE. I have tried many different glues and have found Tandy leather glue to be about the best. This glue bonds leather and suede immediately on contact. The problem is that it comes in liquid form only and has a tendency to run over everything and cannot be removed easily. Rubber cement, which can be bought in any art supply store, works well with some leathers. Actually, you might try any glue that is advertised as working well on leather and suede. I have found that most brands do not live up to the claims, but it is worth a try.

HEAVY CONSTRUCTION PAPER is needed for making patterns. Poster paper is also good for this purpose.

MARKING PEN is used for drawing patterns on the skins.

BUCKLES effectively enhance your belts. They can be found in sewing sections of department stores. Keep an eye out for attractive old buckles from worn-out or no-longer-wanted belts.

NAILHEADS or STUDS are decorations which can be found at Tandy leather shops. The Columbia Button and Nailhead Company (20–26

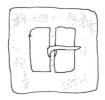

14. *Single-bar buckle*   15. *Center-bar buckle*

Greene Street, New York City 10013) also manufactures a complete line of nailheads.

RIVETS are used mostly for fastening handles to bags and holding buckles on belts. A hardware store might have these.

SNAPS. I prefer the heavy-duty snaps that come in two sizes and also are sold through Tandy. They are available in nickel (silver colored) or brass (gold colored) and are the easiest and strongest snaps to use. Very small snaps are not only too small to be used effectively on leather but they are also a nuisance to handle.

RULER. A 36-inch ruler is necessary if you are planning to make belts. A shorter one is easier to work with for smaller projects. A metal ruler is preferable but a wooden one will be fine.

NEEDLES. Sewing will require the use of a needle or two (depending upon which stitch is being used). These can be needlepoint needles. Glover's needles might also be used.

GAUGE. You may use a draw gauge to cut belts or leather strips. An accurate straight edge must first be cut. The gauge is then fixed for the desired width and, bracing one end on the cut edge, it is pulled the length of the leather. I, personally, do not use this tool, preferring shears for cutting lightweight to medium-weight leather.

4

Leatherwork Techniques

The first and most important rule in starting a leatherwork project is to plan carefully what you are going to do. Measure, punch and cut everything accurately. Careless or hasty preparation means waste of money and leather.

There are several ways to hand-stitch leather. Some of you are probably familiar with the spools of standard thin leather that are obtainable at most hobby shops. This material has been used for stitching by scout troops and in arts and crafts classes, and books are available that teach scout-type stitching. However, I suggest cutting the laces from the skins themselves. This has several advantages over buying pre-cut lacing: the colors of whatever is being made match exactly the colors of the lacing; hand-cut lace is soft, pleasant to touch and attractive, while spooled lacing is hard, thin and splits easily; and cutting your own lacing from the skins costs less.

Lacing (garment sides work best because of their strength even when being cut so thin) should be no thinner than ⅛″ and no wider than ¼″. The difference depends upon how detailed the stitching is to be.

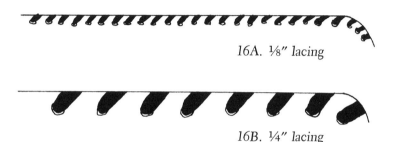

16A. ⅛″ lacing

16B. ¼″ lacing

Cutting the Lacing

Lay the skin flat on the table and, with one continuous movement, cut off the rough edges as shown in Illustration 17. Then, parallel to the new edge, cut your ⅛″ or ³⁄₁₆″ or ¼″ lacing. I prefer to use long lacings, which do not have to be seamed together. Some craftsmen, however, prefer working with shorter 18″ or 24″ laces and, when necessary, add a new piece by overlapping and glueing. If you use a long lacing, be sure to pull it all the way through each hole until the slack is removed. With shorter lace there is no slack. After cutting the lace, stretch it. This will prevent the lace from "giving" once the article has been sewn together and it also tests the lacing for strength. If the lace breaks when stretched, try cutting another lace from another part of the skin. Remember that the belly is the weakest part; cut from another section.

Lacing from Scraps

Don't throw away the small pieces of leather that you think you will not need. They can be made into laces by cutting them into large circles and cutting in a spiral as shown.

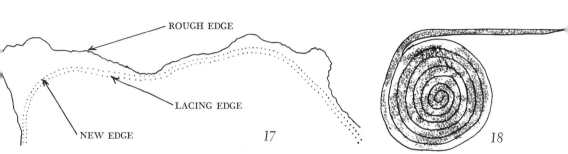

ROUGH EDGE

LACING EDGE

NEW EDGE

17

18

No. 2 LACING

19. Straight stitch

No. 6 LACING

Straight Stitch

The straight stitch is the easiest and quickest way to bind two pieces of leather together. Simply cut the lace, then punch holes (using the number 2 hole for detailed stitching or the number 6 hole for less detailed stitching) ¼″ apart near the edge of the leather as shown in Illustration 19.

Align the holes in the two pieces. Pull the lacing through the first hole, glue down a 1″ tab on the under side, and lace in and out as shown. The lace should be cut at an angle at the end to facilitate its entering each hole. Use the awl to widen each hole slightly if necessary. Lace snugly but not too tight or too loose.

Run your lace all the way around the article. When you come back to where you started, overlap stitches in first three holes (applying just a touch of glue to each of these three stitches) and then cut off the end. If you run out of lace in the middle of your project, cut another strip, overlap the ends 1½″, glue them together and continue. Make sure the lace appears to be a continuous piece.

Cross Stitch

The cross stitch is based on the same procedure as the straight stitch, but the end result is different. Instead of going in every hole, go into every other hole. When the lacing has gone all the way around, turn and repeat in the other direction through the unused holes. When the lacing is finished it should look like Illustration 21.

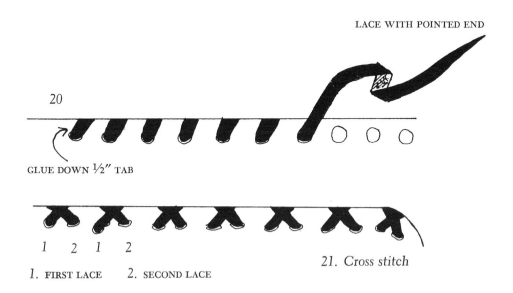

LACE WITH POINTED END

20

GLUE DOWN ½″ TAB

1 *2* *1* *2*

1. FIRST LACE   2. SECOND LACE

21. *Cross stitch*

Contrasting color lacing enhances the work even more, because it adds emphasis to the hand-stitching. I have found that a dark suede—blue, brown, or green—stitched with a light leather lacing—beige, yellow, or red —creates a most pleasing effect.

Bias Stitch

This easy stitch looks like a running stitch in sewing.

22. *Bias stitch*

Saddle Stitch

Two laces are required. The first lace goes up through the first hole and down the second, forming the first stitch. Pull the lace down and back. With the awl, widen the second hole and draw the second lace up through it. Carry the second lace down through the third hole. Widen

23A. Saddle stitch

the third hole with the awl and then pull the first lacing up through this hole. There now should be two stitches on top. Continue this saddle-stitch lacing all the way around and knot at the ends. The underside stitching should look like this:

23B. Underside of saddle stitch

Making a Dart

Handstitched leather darts require a different technique than dressmaker's darts. The saddle stitch is best for making a dart in leather. When you have to shape a garment to fit darts are the solution. Carefully measure the height of the area to be molded and trace the shape of the dart on the wrong side of the leather. (A dart should be elongated with two curved sides, as shown in Illustration 24.) Cut out the center of the dart and

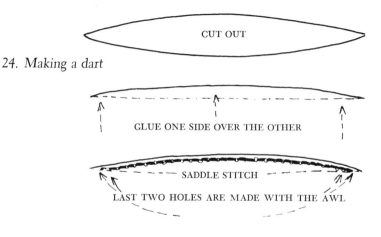

24. Making a dart

CUT OUT

GLUE ONE SIDE OVER THE OTHER

SADDLE STITCH

LAST TWO HOLES ARE MADE WITH THE AWL

discard the leather scrap. Turn the skin over so that the right side is facing up. Bring both curved dart edges together, one overlapping the other, and glue them. Saddle stitch along the dart edge, on the right side of the skin.

Flat Cross Stitch

This is the best stitch for sewing two sections together. Allow the two sides to overlap ½″ and glue them. Use the glue sparingly because even a small amount tends to spread quickly. Punch 2 rows of number 2 holes to look like Illustration 25A.

Starting from the back with 2 strips of lacing, glue down ½″ tab at the end of each and then bring both laces up through the first two holes. The laces now cross each other and go down through the second holes to the underside again. See Illustrations 25B and 25C.

When the stitching is finished, glue down the ½″ tabs and cover both ends on the underside with 1″ squares of leather glued over the tabs.

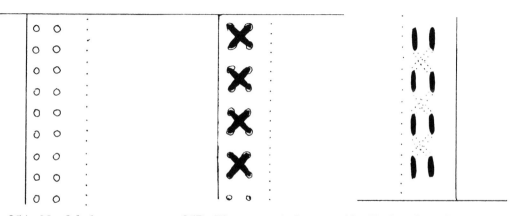

25A. No. 2 holes   25B. Flat cross stitch   25C. Underside of flat cross stitch

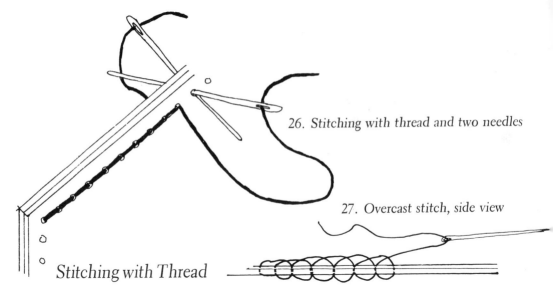

26. Stitching with thread and two needles

27. Overcast stitch, side view

Stitching with Thread

If a more subtle touch is desired, hand stitching with needle and thread is the answer. Two needles are required, thick thread (buttonhole twist will do), and some beeswax. The wax is rubbed on the thread to strengthen the fibers. The saddle stitch is the best to use.

You may also use the overcast stitch. With this only one needle is necessary.

Riveting

Riveting is another method of joining two pieces of leather together. It is usually used when attaching handles to an article. Use a number 4 hole to pierce both layers of leather. Set the top section of the rivet on the two layers and the bottom part of the rivet underneath, then hammer down to fasten the pieces together.

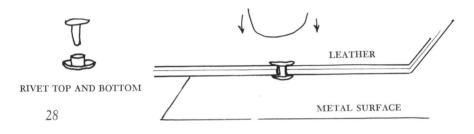

RIVET TOP AND BOTTOM

LEATHER

METAL SURFACE

28

Old habits die hard. Try to stop thinking in inches (although that is the unit of measurement used in this book), and purchase a centimeter ruler. The metric system is much easier to use. The United States is switching to the metric system in the coming years so it might be well to familiarize yourselves with it.

Studs

Studs, or nailheads, have been used since medieval times for the decoration of leather saddles and harnesses. Today, their bright, shiny appearance has made them popular on belts, bags, and clothing. Of the many types available, I find the 2-pronged stud the most convenient to use. The 4-, 5-, and 6-pronged types come with shorter prongs and require much more work to put into place.

4-PRONGED

29. Nailheads or studs   2-PRONGED

Studs come in many different sizes, from about ⅛" to about ¾" in diameter. Some are shaped as stars, pyramids or animals, and can be used just as readily as ordinary round studs.

Before using studs on a belt, you must establish the spacing between them. Each size stud requires different spacing. For example, you may wish to use ½" studs. Place one stud on the edge of the belt pattern, with the prongs parallel to the edge. It should be upside down and look like Illustration 30.

30

2-PRONGED STUD   EVERY ½"

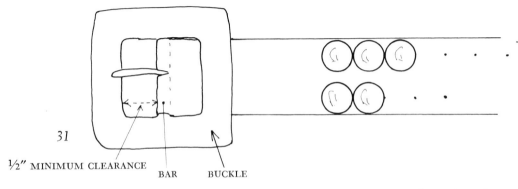

31

½″ MINIMUM CLEARANCE   BAR   BUCKLE

Measure the distance from the edge of the pattern to the point where the prong is to enter the leather. Draw a line parallel to the edge at this point and put a mark every ½″ along this line. Punch out the marks on the pattern; these holes are where the stud prongs will go. Use the smallest-sized punch hole. Studded belts need a buckle that has at least a ½″ space between the bar and the buckle for easy clearance. Begin studding an inch or two from the buckle.

Eyelets

Eyelets are used on belts and bags to prevent holes from stretching out of shape. Punch a number 3 hole in the desired position. Position the eyelet in the hole and, with an eyelet setter, simply squeeze. The setter will spread the core of the eyelet and secure it. See Illustration 13.

Snaps

Heavy-duty snaps are very useful. They come in two sizes, both requiring a snap setter and a small anvil. If you cannot find an anvil, a small spoon can be used instead. Illustration 32 shows how to set the snaps.

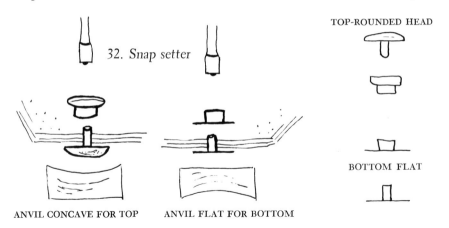

32. Snap setter

TOP-ROUNDED HEAD

BOTTOM FLAT

ANVIL CONCAVE FOR TOP   ANVIL FLAT FOR BOTTOM

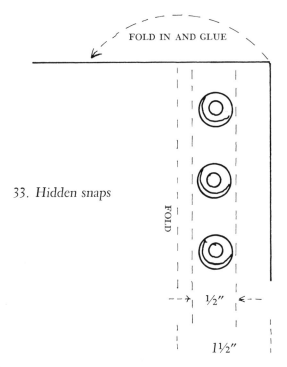

FOLD IN AND GLUE

FOLD

33. *Hidden snaps*

½″

1½″

Hidden snaps may be applied to trousers or a jacket. When cutting, an extra 1½″ must be allowed at the edge of the garment where the snaps are to be applied.

A ½″ strip of suede is glued down the center of the wrong side of the 1½″ flap as reinforcement.

The snaps are now set along the suede strip at regular intervals with the snap heads on the underside. The whole 1½″ band is turned in and glued flat, concealing the snap heads.

The bottom halves of the snaps are inserted in corresponding positions on the other side of the garment.

Staining

You may want to darken the natural light color of heavy cowhide. This is done by staining with commercial leather dye. Leather shoe dyes, available in shoe repair shops, are also suitable. Apply the dye to the clean, dry leather with a soft cloth. Work the dye in until the desired color is attained and then buff off any excess. If you use a liquid dye, apply it, wipe off the excess, and then rub in a leather preservative. This prevents the dye from rubbing off. If the edges of a cowhide article need finishing, mix equal parts of dye, glue, and water and apply the solution to the edges of the leather with a dauber or soft cloth.

Tooling

Tooling is the applying of designs to leather. Thin leather is not suited to this technique, but heavy cowhide (4- to 6-ounce) is. Draw the pattern for your design on a thin piece of paper. The design can be very simple and geometric or as ornate as you wish. Take a sponge and dampen the entire surface of the leather. This will prevent the possibility of water staining. The leather should be damp but not wet. Place the pattern on the damp leather and, with an ordinary pencil, trace the pattern. This will leave a soft impression in the leather. After this is done take a modeling tool and deepen the lines of the pattern with smooth, firm strokes. These will remain after the leather is dry. A ruler will help for long straight lines.

The tooled lines can now be left as they are or other effects can be added. With the aid of a hammer and using any one of several stamping tools available from leathercraft or hobby stores, you can stamp shading, stars, curves, and flowers onto the leather. A patterned background emphasizes the original design.

For tooling, use only vegetable-tanned or bark-tanned cowhide. Chrome-tanned cowhide does not absorb moisture and therefore isn't suitable for tooling.

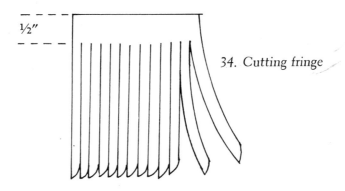

34. Cutting fringe

Fringe

Fringe may be added to jacket sleeves, trouser legs or bags—in three different ways. You can add a section as the garment is being stitched together, or you can extend the pattern to allow for as many inches as you want to be fringed. Another method is to make a line of number 1 holes at the edge to be fringed. Take a length of lace, cut it to the desired fringe lengths, knot one end. Pass the unknotted end through a hole. A small glass bead can be added on the other side to hold the fringe in place.

Glueing and Stitching

In making almost any object it becomes necessary to join at least two layers of leather. This is accomplished first by glueing, and then by stitching in holes made with a drive punch. When applying glue from a squeeze tube onto the leather, be sure you control the glue and not vice versa. Glue tends to run onto the leather very rapidly. The white, liquid glue that Tandy manufactures is the best bonding glue. However, it will not come off if you spill some on a sueded leather. If this does happen (it usually will) you can try to sand it off with fine sandpaper. In some cases this will remove the glue without leaving a mark. When glueing leather to suede or leather to leather, sandpaper all the areas that are to be glued. This roughs up the leather surface and helps the glue to bond. Apply the glue evenly over all seams or areas to be glued. The glue has only to be placed on one side of the article. When the white glue begins to sink into the leather and appears tacky (this should take one minute) put both sides of the leather

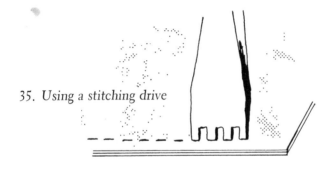

35. Using a stitching drive

together, pressing lightly. Allow another minute to pass and then press very hard or hit gently with a hammer.

Zippers

Heavy-duty zippers are best for leather. Zippers are used for all kinds of bags. Before glueing and stitching the zipper to the leather, the stitch holes must be punched in the leather. The glue is then applied to the leather over the holes. The zipper is placed on the leather and pressed down. Needle and thread are used to stitch the zipper. You can use flat cross stitch or saddle stitch. Do not punch holes in the zipper.

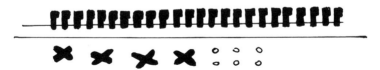

36. Stitching a zipper

Skiving

Skiving is a method of reducing the thickness of leather by paring the wrong side with a razor knife. If thick leather is to be flexed—as around a buckle—the area to fold must be thinned or skived. It must be done carefully and gradually in order not to cut through the leather. Be careful not to slice clear through the skin.

Finishes and Conditioners

Excluding suede, the look and life of any leather will be improved with some form of finish. The finish can be applied to natural finish or dyed leathers. The conditioner softens and preserves the leather. The same high quality products that can be purchased for shoes work well on good quality skins. Some finishes, such as "Lexol" or saddle soap, will add a darker, richer tone. Saddle soap is worked into a lather with a little water and daubed on the leather with a sponge. After drying the article is buffed with a clean cloth. Neutral-colored shoe wax leaves a nice finish on most leathers.

Every design in this book will improve with age, use, and normal treatment. Pastel suede is difficult to keep clean, but you can try commercial suede cleaner. Fine sandpaper may also be used to scrub off dirt.

Painting on Leather

This can be done by using waterproof markers or acrylic paints. No preparation of the leather is required.

Handles

Illustration 38 shows a few different styles of handles. A strip of thin leather should be placed inside all handles for added strength. On the inside of each bag, where the rivets are to be hammered, a 2″ square of

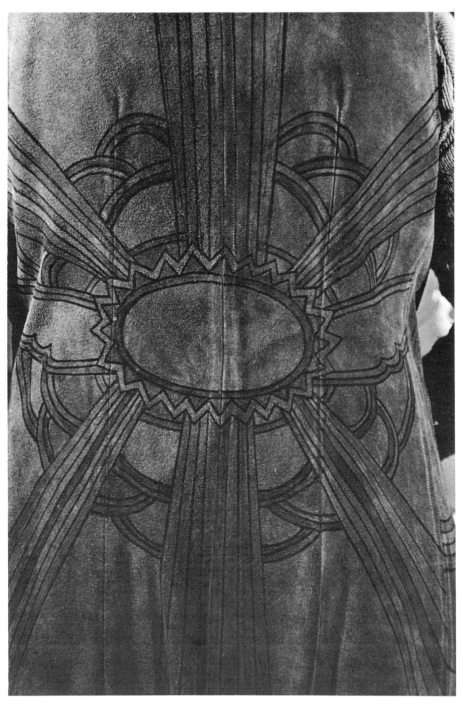

37. A painted design by Phyllis Krim.

leather should be added also to strengthen the bag. Shoulder straps should be made the same way as the handles. A buckle might be added to the shoulder strap for adjusting length. An inside strip of leather should be included in any shoulder strap.

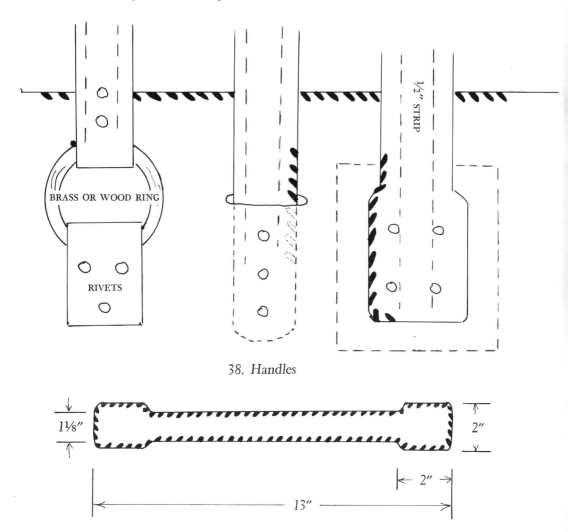

38. Handles

39. This 15th-century suit of Japanese armor is made of innumerable strips of hardened leather held together with leather stitching. The drawing to the right shows the construction details. The strips are about ¾″ wide. This construction method might be used for a more ambitious project. Eight- or ten-ounce latigo cowhide would be needed for the strips, and garment cowhide for the lacing. The edges of the strips have to be finished. They can run from 3″ to 15″ in length. Every one or two inches there must be a row of lacing for support.

40

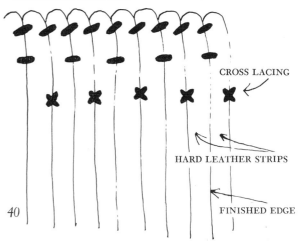

CROSS LACING

HARD LEATHER STRIPS

FINISHED EDGE

5

Belts

Besides being something to hold up one's pants, a belt can be a smart fashion accessory. A hand-crafted belt is more attractive than a pre-cut, machined one, and you have the pleasure of knowing you made it yourself.

Suede is preferable to smooth leather for belts because the glue adheres better to the rougher surface. You will need a piece of suede that is at least twice as big as the finished belt.

Before beginning to draw on the skins, you must prepare a pattern. This should be made of "oak tag" or heavy poster paper. If the pattern is longer than the paper, tape two or more pieces together. The pattern is the same for a hand-stitched or a studded belt, but once the leather has been cut the procedure is slightly different for each style.

First, determine waist size. Let us say it is a 30" waist. Next, measure the length of the buckle bar. This will determine the width of the belt.

On the pattern paper, 1½" from the edge, draw a line the length of the buckle bar (Illustration 42B). Place the buckle on the paper with its bar over the bar line just drawn. Make a mark at the inner edge of the buckle frame (Illustration 42C). Measure thirty inches to the right of this mark, and make a second mark. Since this marks the belt average of 30",

now make marks at 29″, 31″ and 32″. These will be the locations of the belt holes (Illustration 43A).

Allow an additional 5″ to the right of the 32″ mark for the tab of the belt. At the center of the 32″ mark draw a vertical line the length of your buckle bar (Illustration 43B). To determine the top edge of the belt, draw a line from the top point of the buckle bar through the top point of the line at the 32″ mark and extending 5″ past it. Connect the lower points the same way.

Draw a line from the top of the buckle-bar line to the left edge of the pattern paper (1½″ from the buckle bar line) at a slight inward angle. Do the same from the bottom point. This makes a tapered buckle flap. See Illustration 43C.

Following the pattern, with a razor knife or shears and a ruler, cut out the belt, rounding off the tab end.

The studded belt pattern is not complete until all the stud holes have been carefully measured and punched on the paper pattern. Begin measuring for the holes 2″ from the buckle bar. After the pattern has been cut out, place it on the underside of the leather and trace around it. Make a mark in each punched hole for the studs. With shears, carefully cut out the belt. It is advisable to practice cutting on some leather scraps before attempting to cut the belt. Just draw a few straight lines and practice cutting them. Do this until every line you cut is absolutely straight and even. With a hole punch, punch out each marked stud hole. Use the number 1 (smallest) hole on the punch. Turn the punch at every hole, it will cut better. When you have finished punching the holes, put in the studs.

Fold the belt at the buckle-bar line and, if the buckle has a tongue, cut a ½″ slit at the center of the fold. Slip the tapered flap through the buckle

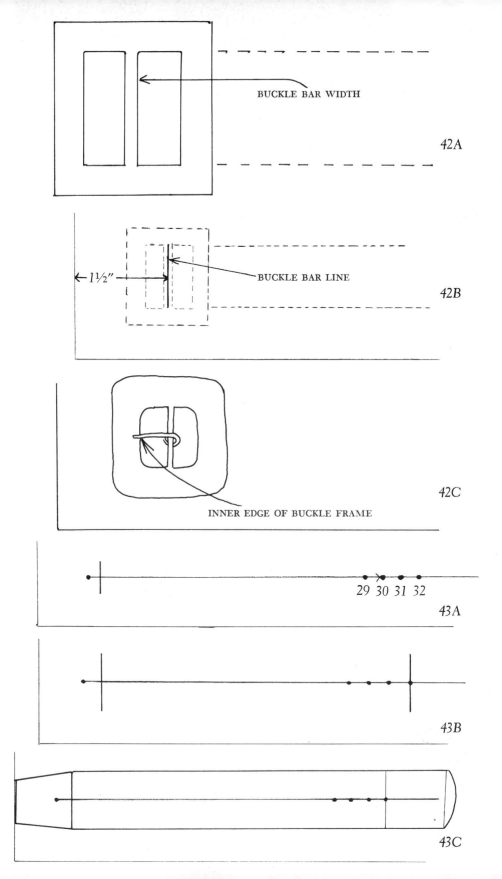

BUCKLE BAR WIDTH

42A

←— 1½″ —→ BUCKLE BAR LINE

42B

INNER EDGE OF BUCKLE FRAME

42C

29 30 31 32

43A

43B

43C

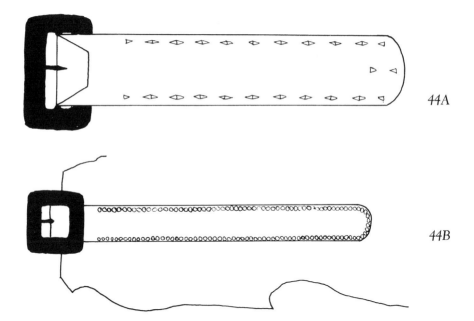

44A

44B

and pass the buckle tongue through the slit. Fold the flap over and glue down. The back of the belt should look like Illustration 44A.

Spread glue around the edges and in the center of the back of the belt, except for ½″ near the buckle. (Don't use too much glue. It may spread and ruin your work.) Press the belt on the remaining piece of leather firmly so the glue will hold. Cut around the belt carefully. Insert the eyelets in their proper places. (Illustration 44B.)

Hand-stitched Belt

For a hand-stitched belt, place the pattern on the skin and trace around it. Cut it out and attach the buckle as described above. Spread glue on the underside of the belt and press it to the remaining skin. After allowing a few minutes for it to dry, cut it out. At ½″ intervals, ⅛″ from the edge, punch holes, using number 3 size on the hole punch. If a smaller pattern is preferred, punch holes closer together, using a number 1 or 2 hole. Punch the holes the entire length of the belt. Cut leather strips and lace the edges with whatever stitch you chose. Punch and place eyelets for the buckle holes.

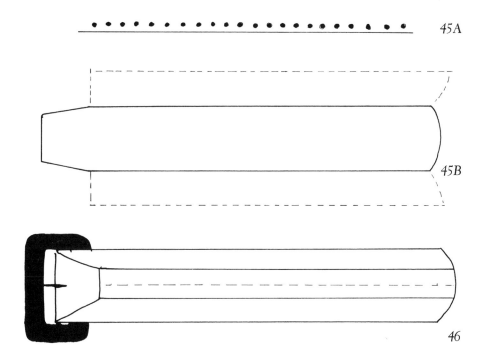

45A

45B

46

Finished-edge Belt

If you are going to make a finished-edge belt, add an extra ½″ on each long side of the pattern when designing. Place the pattern on the leather, trace around it, and cut. Attach the buckle, fold and glue the two long flaps the length of the belt. Glue a strip of suede down the center of the back— wide enough to extend over the edges of both flaps. Use Elmer's glue, mixed with dye, along the end to bond it. Punch out buckle holes and set in the eyelets.

Another way to make a finished-edge belt is to cut out the pattern, as above. Then make another pattern to the desired width of the finished belt. Cut this out of suede. Fold and glue the long side edges of the main part of the belt as in Illustration 46. Glue the suede belt lining down the center of the belt back starting ½″ from the buckle-bar slit. This is a good method for working with thin snakeskins.

Braid Belt

Very attractive thin braid belts, chokers, and wristbands can be made by cutting three very thin 3 ounce laces (⅛″ wide for extra thin and ¼″ wide for just very thin) and braiding them together. The ends can be knotted and left as fringe, or the entire belt can be backed to keep the loose ends in place, so that snaps or a buckle can be added. You must cut the lacings twice as long as the finished belt. The closing can be either snaps or a small buckle.

48. This belt is brown suede with brown cowhide lace. The handmade buckle is sterling silver. Cross-stitching at the edges (using a No. 1 punch) holds the suede to the latigo lining.

49. This studded belt has no real buckle or overlap. The two nailheads in the center are snaps. Four snap bottoms are attached to the other end of the belt. The belt can then have a range of five

sizes. The square self "buckle" has been reinforced with 4-ounce latigo glued to the lining. The ¼″ studs were mounted on two ¾″ strips of red leather and glued to the lining. A blue leather braid was glued along the center.

50. A kelly green belt with red python center inset. The center pattern for the ⅜″ nickel nailheads was made with a compass. The larger nailheads are ⅝″. Three laces form the closing at the back.

51. A 1¼″-wide red goatskin studded belt with a nickel buckle. The nickel studs are ⅛″. A rectangular pattern of studs occurs every few inches.

52. A 2″-wide studded belt with a cast nickel buckle and ⅝″ nickel studs. A blue cowhide bias stitch in No. 4 holes runs along the center. This is done before the lining is attached.

53. This burnt-orange calfskin belt has an American Indian silver-and-turquoise buckle. The belt has a finished edge and is ¾″ wide.

54. A 1½″-wide brown garment cowhide belt, with a cast nickel buckle, ⅝″ nickel studs, and a suede lining.

55. A 1½″-wide finished-edge tan python belt with a cast nickel buckle.

56. A 2″-wide belt with rivets and lacing, made of 8-ounce latigo cowhide dyed brown. Near the edge is a bias-stitch trim of brown cowhide (No. 4 hole). Brass rings form the buckle, and medium gold rivets were used.

PHOTOS BY PETER POLYMENAKOS

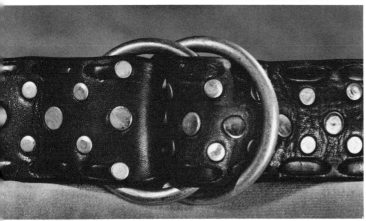

57. These belts were made out of antique sashes from Afghanistan, glued to a lining of garment cowhide and cross-stitched all the way around. Each belt closes with two small straps and buckles, riveted into place. The small straps are also lined and stitched for strength.

R. K. FURST

6

Bags

A few summers ago, I was planning a European vacation and needed a flight bag. On several forays to local luggage shops and department stores I found only two types of bags. Those made of imported leather or suede were attractive, well constructed, and also outrageously expensive. The vinyl or canvas bags were less costly, but they had a somewhat limited life expectancy. I have a habit of becoming unreasonably attached to certain simple material possessions that I own, and I wanted a bag that would hold together for a while. I have also had the memorable experience of having a store-bought machine-stitched bag fall apart at an airport check-in counter. Ultimately, I made my own flight bag, and after a couple of years of continuous daily use, it still looks new.

In this chapter, patterns and photographs will show how to make bags that are attractive and stylish. They should also hold together for quite some time. My first flight bag is practical in a variety of different situations. The soft construction allows it to be swung over a shoulder for everyday use. The handles on the sides instantly convert the bag to a very roomy "weekender" or carryall. It can be made in conservative colors or a lively color combina-

58. Flight bag

59. Pocketbook

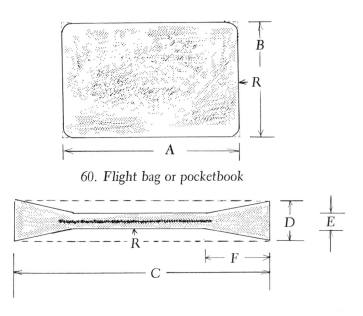

60. *Flight bag or pocketbook*

tion. Patterns are provided to make this bag in two sizes. The smaller size is intended to be used as a pocketbook.

Patterns for a Flightbag and a Pocketbook

	FLIGHTBAG	POCKETBOOK
	MEASUREMENTS ARE IN INCHES.	
A	35	22
B	20	12
C	45	28
D	7	3½
E	3	2½
F	12	7
zipper	22	12

The pattern for the center has been provided with an extra inch or two to allow for stretching. When glueing the two sections together, cut away the extra piece. Line up the two points R and start glueing toward the bottom of the bag from there.

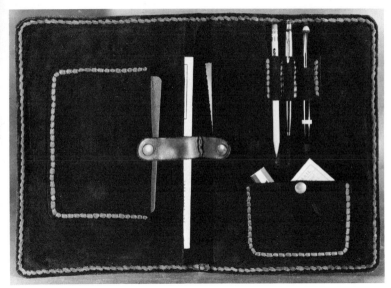

61. Attaché case: inside

62. Attaché case: outside

Attaché Case

The case (see Photographs 61 and 62) was made from 6-ounce latigo cowhide. The interior has a full suede pocket on each side with smaller pockets stitched onto these. The snaps which are secured to the pockets help to keep papers neat. The bag was made using the saddle stitch with garment cowhide lacing. Straight or cross stitches can also be used. The exterior of the bag has been dyed a mellow brown. The interior is chocolate brown suede. The lacing is dark tan cowhide. The case can be made in a number of different sizes. Measurements are:

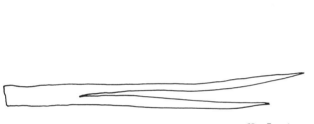

63. Lacing

QUANTITY	DESCRIPTION	SIZE (IN INCHES)
1	exterior cowhide	12½ by 19
2	suede pockets	12½ by 10
1	suede pocket	6 by 7
1	suede pocket	4 by 5
1	center support (suede)	12½ by 4
1	center strap (optional)	1 by 4
1	suede pen holder	2 by 3

Fold back and glue down a 1″ edge on all four sides of each pocket piece. Glue the small pockets along the edge to the larger ones and stitch. Glue the penholder into place along the short edges.

Split the lacing down the middle, all the way to within ½″ of the end, leaving a small tab. Stitch the small pockets down, starting and ending with the end tabs glued to the underside of the suede. When you have finished stitching, glue a 1″ square of leather on top of the tab and the lacing ends to secure them.

Glue the suede support strip to the wrong side of the latigo, along the center fold.

Now glue the inside pockets into position on the latigo, and punch all sewing holes along the outer edge of the case.

Glue the lacing tab at the center edge of the support strip. Thread one end of the split strip through to the right side of the case, and begin saddle stitching (see Illustration 26). When you reach the end tab, punch holes through it and lace it down.

If you want the center strap with the snaps, cut this out (1″ by 4″ latigo). Attach the snaps. Stitch the strap through the case at the center fold.

A Handbag

This slim bag can be made in a variety of colors and sizes and with different handles. As far as leather appliqués, the design possibilities are unlimited.

I made the thin plywood handles shown, but leather ones will work just as well. Three extra suede pieces were cut to fit the slits in the handle and, before the center support was added to the bag, three corresponding slits were cut at the top fold of the bag. Then each extra suede piece was inserted through its place in the handle and stitched down flat to both sides of its corresponding slit in the bag. I used the cross stitch to hold the two sides together and flat cross-stitching to seam the Aztec temple design together. Overall, the bag measures 10″ by 12″. Blue turquoise leather was used for the center section; salmon-colored leather for the bottom section. Snaps are used to close the flap; a buckle could have been used to close it.

Each piece of the colored design sections should be overlapped ½″ over the piece below it, as shown in Illustration 64B. Remember this in cutting the sections to be appliquéd. In stitching them to the bag, start ½″ in to allow space for a neat final stitch.

Glue the support to the back as shown in Illustration 64A.

Glue the front and back together and stitch.

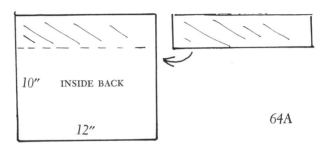

10″   INSIDE BACK

12″

64A

PETER POLYMENAKOS

The pieces needed to construct the thin "envelope" bag are:

QUANTITY	DESCRIPTION	SIZE (IN INCHES)
1	suede or cowhide back	12 by 12
1	suede or cowhide front	12 by 10
1	center support	12 by 4
2	baby snaps	

64B

½″ OVERLAP

Passport Wallet

A passport wallet can also serve as an eyeglass holder. It is designed to hang around the neck. When traveling, it is always wise to have your passport with you. I do not like to carry a bag all the time and in warm weather there are no adequate pockets on light clothing. This wallet solves the problem. Suspended around the neck and worn either outside or inside a jacket or shirt it keeps your passport, money and keys handy. It is also a very good theft-prevention device, if worn concealed.

These bags can be appliquéd with patch designs or they can be left plain. They can be made in suede, or garment cowhide, lined snakeskin, or any light strong leather. If a design is to be made on the front, the front panel should be lined with a thin leather. The strap can be braided, or folded and glued leather or a super-thin stitched strap. The length of the strap should be just long enough to reach around the head of the wearer. It can be fastened to the bag either by small rivets or by stitching. The dimensions of the bag are 4½″ by 6¼″. The back side dimensions are 4½″ by 7½″. The extra 1¼″ on the back is turned in and glued down. This acts as a reinforcement for the rivets or stitching. Glue two sides and the bottom along the edges. Stitch together, starting at the top of one side and when you get back to the top continue to stitch only the single thickness of the front. Cross stitching works best. Two varieties of decoration are shown on page 66.

Cross-stitch Wallet

This small bag is chocolate brown with leather lacing. It will serve as a small secretary or wallet. It has a lining of Chinese silk. There are two

R. K. FURST

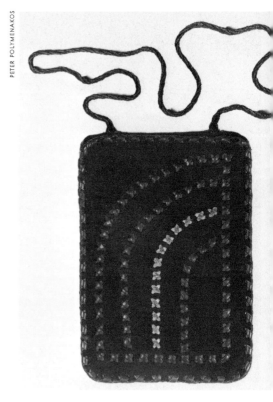

PETER POLYMENAKOS

67 and 68. Passport wallets, alternate designs

thin leather pockets with a card pocket on one side and a pen holder on the other. The measurements are as follows:

QUANTITY	DESCRIPTION	SIZE (IN INCHES)
1	exterior piece	11 by 7½
1	thin leather lining or fabric lining	11 by 7½
2	pockets	7½ by 5½
1	card pocket	4½ by 4
1	pen pocket	2 by 1½

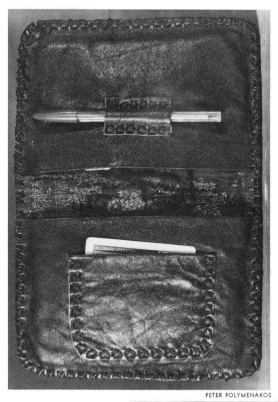

69. *Cross-stitch wallet: inside*

70. *Cross-stitch wallet: outside*

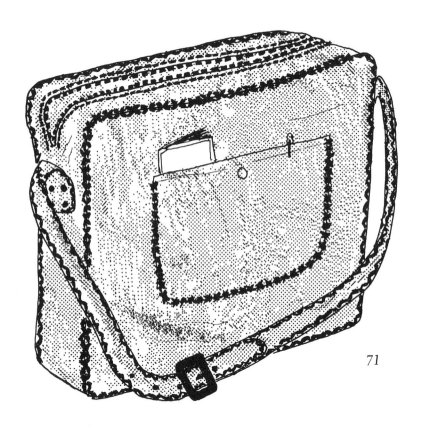

71

Everything was cross-stitched together. The design is flat-crossed and the pockets are flat-crossed. Two small ½″ by 3″ tabs were placed at the center edges to reinforce the fabric. Suede split would be fine for the exterior and a light cabretta would make unbulky pockets.

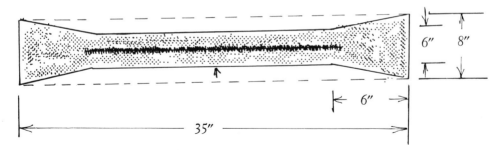

72. Bag for bowling, school or shopping

8″ × 15¾″ PIECE OF PLYWOOD OR MASONITE FOR BASE

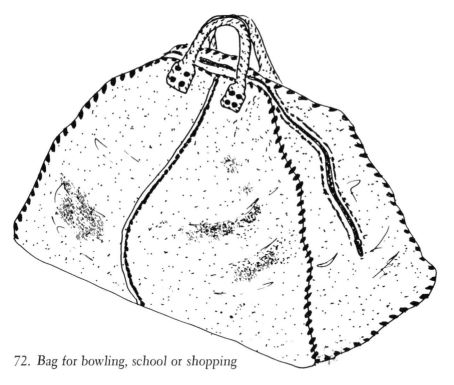

24″ ZIPPER

7″ 16″

8″

36″

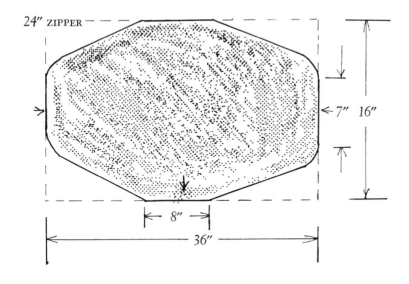

6″ 8″

6″

35″

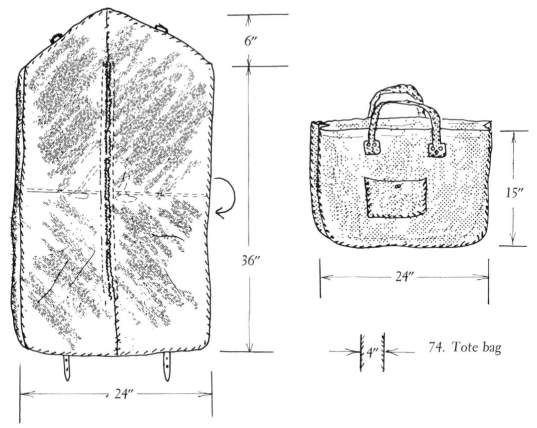

6"

36"

24"

73. Folding garment bag

15"

24"

4"

74. Tote bag

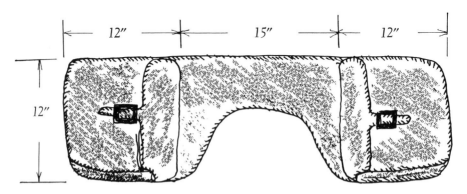

12" 15" 12"

12"

75. Saddle bag for motorcycles and bicycles

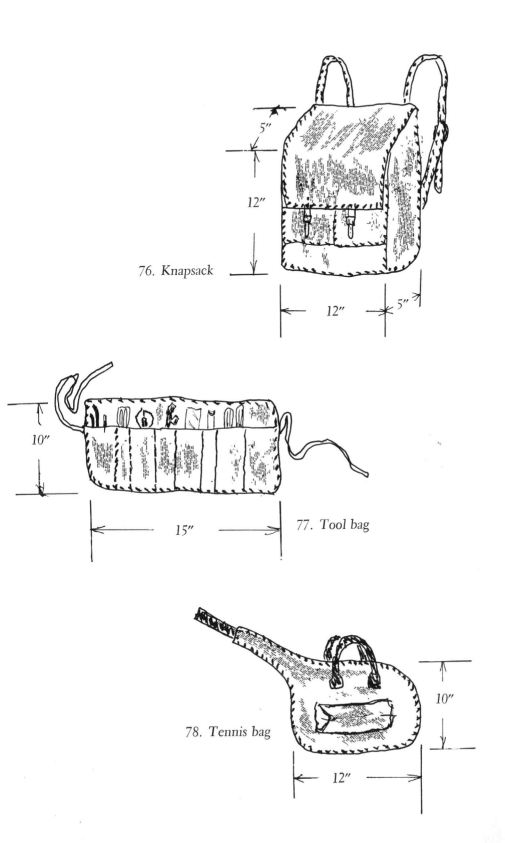

76. Knapsack

5"

12"

12" 5"

10"

15" 77. Tool bag

78. Tennis bag

10"

12"

7

Environmental Projects

Leather as a creative medium has strong tactile qualities. What other material is so seductive to the touch? And this quality can be brought out by the way you design and work with leather. Unlike some other materials, leather can be widely useful and pleasureable.

A chair or a couch, covered with fabric, might look attractive but re-upholstering your present furniture or covering cushions with leather or suede will dramatically transform your environment.

A plain coat or dress, when made of leather, might become an exquisite piece of clothing. Clean lines and simplicity of design are the key words in creating leather garments. Choose a design that is not faddish but will continue to please you for years to come.

Ideas can come from many different sources. Your own environment, occupation, hobbies and tastes will be factors in deciding what to make. Always be sure to measure properly, and leave a ½″ seam anywhere that two pieces of leather are to be joined together. Here are some suggestions.

Additional Projects

aprons
artist portfolios
bedspreads
book jackets
camera bags
capes
chairs
chaps
checkbook covers
chokers
coats
cushions
dog leashes
dresses
fishing rod cases

gloves
guitar cases
gym bags
halters
hats
jackets
magazine racks
meditation pil-
 lows
organizers
pillows
plant holders
school bags
shirts
shorts

skirts
slippers
sofas
suit bags
tank tops
tennis racket
 covers
ties
tool bags
tote bags
trousers
typewriter covers
wall hangings
watchbands

Wall Organizers

These can be made in many different sizes and shapes. An artist might like one with lots of long, thin pockets for brushes. For office use, an organizer with pockets for standard-size stationery would be practical. You will need a ¼″ dowel, or similar-type rod, for your top support, in the same width as your organizer. Dowels can be obtained in a hobby shop or a lumber yard. See following pages.

79. Wall organizer
R. K. FURST

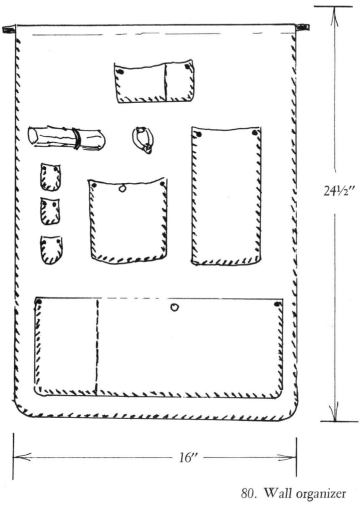

24½"

16"

80. Wall organizer

Pillows

Photograph 82 shows two pillows of suede patchwork designs inspired by the Appalachian quilt makers of the 1890's. The front and back are joined with cross stitching. The patchwork is joined with flat cross stitch-

81A. Patchwork squares and pattern variations

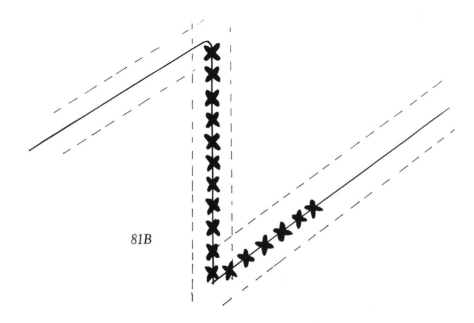

81B

82. *Pillows*

ing. Behind each seam is a thin strip of leather ¾" wide. As shown in Illustration 81B, each patch is glued halfway on the strip. Then the other is joined. The two are now cross stitched together. Broken line represents strip on underside.

The stitching calls for the number 1 punch. The pillow can be filled with foam rubber, feathers or kapok. Stitch together the entire front design, then stitch it to the back on three sides. Put the pillow inside and stitch the remaining side closed. Now finish stitching in the other direction for the cross stitch to be complete.

Here are four different patchwork designs, each of which was created by rearranging in different patterns a 45-degree triangle. The repetition of form creates a stunning visual effect for pillows, bags, or bedspreads. If you

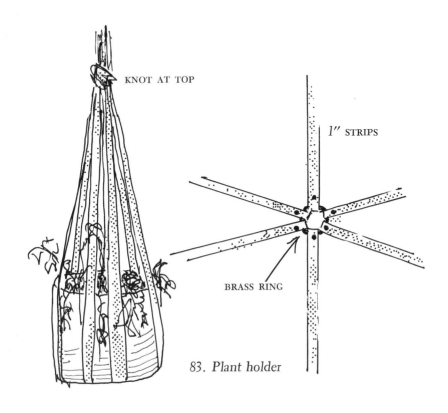

KNOT AT TOP

1″ STRIPS

BRASS RING

83. Plant holder

use a machine, a backing strip behind each patch would not be needed. The designs may be executed using only two colors or by using light shades where the white is and dark shades where the dark triangles are. The patch size can measure anywhere from 1″ to as large as 6″, 8″, or 10″ but 5″ is a good practical size. On a piece of heavy paper, draw two 5″ lines at right angles to one another. Connect the two ends with a diagonal and cut out. This is the pattern.

The drawings and photographs on pages 80 through 83 are excellent examples of leather articles for personal use or for striking decorative effect.

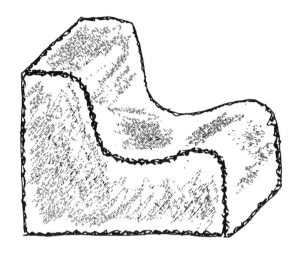

84. Foam chair covered in suede

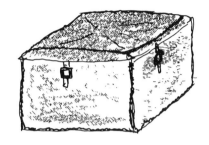

85. Hassock

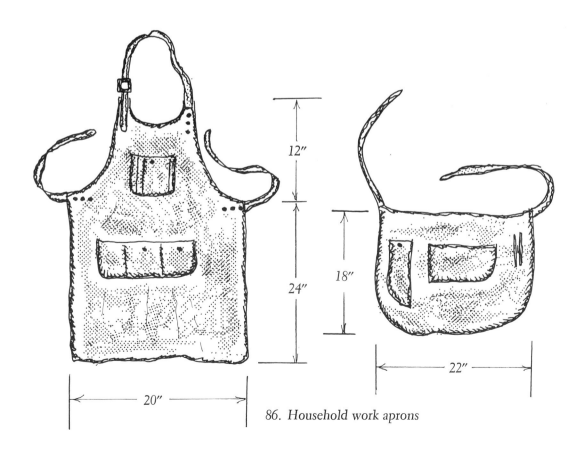

86. Household work aprons

87. The Bastiano lounge (opposite top), designed by Tobia Scarpa, has soft leather cushions on a wood frame. It epitomizes comfort, good design and quality in materials and workmanship seldom seen today.

88, 89. The classic beauty of suede and leather for furniture is apparent in these chrome-tube frame designs by Mies van der Rohe (opposite bottom and above). This furniture, called "modern" and esteemed for its superior design and sleek beauty, was designed in the mid-1920s.

8

Clothes

Clothes made from leather should be well fitted and simply designed in order to be practical and effective. Avoid darts and frills. These do not translate well to leather. Do not use patterns suitable to stretch fabric or knits. Leather will not stretch.

Handmade leather clothes, when properly constructed with detailed stitching, will last for many years. Choose patterns and styles which avoid any kind of "faddy" fashions. Styles that last year after year are the designs to use for leather.

You can copy a favorite piece of clothing as long as it is suitable to leather. If you do not want to take the garment apart, you can copy it by measuring it very carefully and making a paper pattern. Or, if it is old enough (perhaps a pair of jeans), take it apart and copy it on pattern paper. Be sure each piece lies flat before drawing. Cut carefully, allowing ½" for each seam. Always be sure that everything has been measured accurately before cutting. You can also use dressmakers' patterns put out by various companies. These vary greatly in price. Be careful not to choose a pattern with too numerous or complicated pieces. Follow the instructions for assembling very carefully.

90. A true leather-lover of the past: Buffalo Bill Cody resplendent in his frontier work clothes—leather jacket, pants, boots, gloves, bag, belt and hat.

Since leather is a rather expensive material to work with, it is advisable first to make a muslin pattern, basted together by hand. Any alterations should be made on the muslin. An old bed sheet can also be used to make a pattern.

When you have the finished pattern, lay all pieces on the skins, making sure there is enough room all around. Parts of the garment susceptible to the most tension or wear should be cut if possible from the center back of the leather.

Pants

You can buy a commercially made pants pattern—one specified as being suitable for leatherwork—or you can create your own pattern from pants you already own.

To make a pair of leather pants from a pair of jeans, without taking them apart, proceed as follows.

Lay down one front pants leg on pattern paper and trace it. Outline the tracing to allow an extra ½″ all the way around for the outside seam. Turn the pants leg over and trace a pattern of the back section of the leg the same way. You will need one left front, one right front, one left back and one right back. It is a good idea to mark, on the right side of your pattern pieces, "left front" or "left back." This avoids mistakes later when cutting the leather. No seam allowance is needed on the back pants leg.

For the waistband, a 1″ seam allowance must be included. For example, a 1½″ finished waistband requires a 2½″ strip of leather. You will also need belting or fabric lining.

91

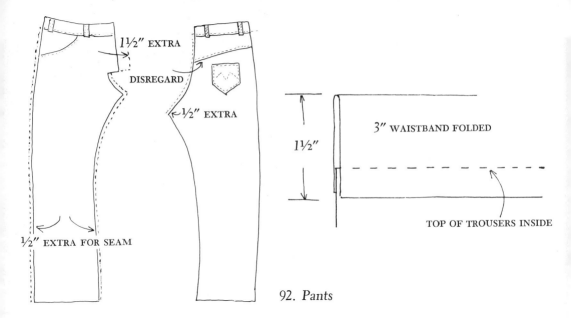

1½″ EXTRA

DISREGARD

½″ EXTRA

1½″

3″ WAISTBAND FOLDED

TOP OF TROUSERS INSIDE

½″ EXTRA FOR SEAM

92. Pants

Cut out the pattern pieces, trace them on the wrong side of the leather (transferring identifying marks to the wrong side) and cut out the leather.

In putting the garment sections together, it is a good idea to follow the construction sequence as given in a dressmaker's pattern, unless you feel you can proceed with confidence. The simplest way to attach a waistband is to insert the top edge of the belt approximately 1″ between the folded waistband piece and then glue and stitch through all layers. Flat cross stitching or saddle stitching is best for pants. Hidden snaps may be applied to the fly front or you can stitch in a zipper. Even lacing may be used if you wish. Patch pockets and belt loops can be added. Pockets should have a ½″ flap glued down around all edges for reinforcement.

Skirt

The skirt opposite was made in forest green reversible garment leather (suede side out) and in natural chamois pieces patched together. It is unlined in the leather version. A 4″ cotton facing was sewn at the waist of the fragile chamois skirt. The skirt can be made from garment cowhide, chamois, suede or calfskin. There is a 7″ zipper in the back. The stitching is either bias, cross or saddle. The effect can be either casual and utilitarian or elegant.

93 94

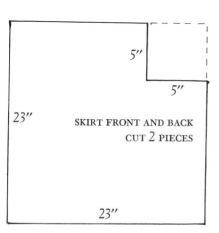

5"

5"

23"

SKIRT FRONT AND BACK
CUT 2 PIECES

23"

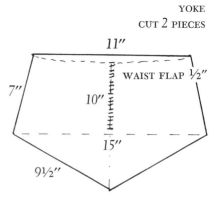

YOKE
CUT 2 PIECES

11"

7"

WAIST FLAP ½"

10"

15"

9½"

95. Pattern for skirt (misses' size 8)

96. Jacket of dark brown garment cowhide. Howard made it using an old blue-jean jacket as the pattern. It was simplified to just six pieces: the two halves of the back, the two halves of the front, and two sleeves. A small cadet collar was added. Flat cross-stitching was used throughout, and snaps were used for the closing. Snaps were also used in the bag shown instead of a zipper.

97. Lisa made this star-studded extravaganza just for fun. It is pink cabretta with metallic silver stars and studs. There is a thin cotton lining to prevent the lightweight leather from stretching. The pattern is a standard notion-counter pattern adapted to leather.

98. This jacket was made from reversible garment cowhide, suede side out. A facing

was used for the collar and lapels so that they, too, would be suede. The lapels and collar are straight-stitched and all seams and pockets are saddle-stitched, as reinforcement for the thin leather. Darts at the waist enhance the fit.

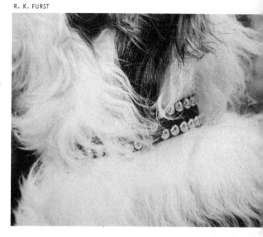

99, 100. Two very simple and incredibly lovely tunics. The light one is of supersoft chamois, the dark one of deerskin. These garments are loose-fitting. An old shirt or jacket can serve as a pattern.

101. After wearing this collar in Central Park one recent Sunday afternoon, Daryl, a strapping young English sheepdog, received no less than three phone calls from vivacious young French poodles inquiring about his plans for the next weekend.

Postscript

A craftsman in any medium must have a thorough understanding and appreciation of the materials involved. With its sensuous texture and great potential for brilliant or subdued color interaction, soft leather should inspire the craftsperson to delightful harmonies and daring combinations. Ignore the dictates of fashion and make honest efforts to create your own original designs. By selecting only high quality, beautiful skins and executing techniques carefully and patiently—with real affection for the material —the results will be work you will be proud of. The creator of a ten-minute, dyed latigo bag held together with five stitches should be embarrassed to call his work handcraftsmanship.

Keep in mind that when working only with shears and punch, a project can move anywhere with you, to be enjoyed outdoors in the country or anytime during a long journey. The way has been shown, feel free to innovate and experiment. Most important of all, have fun.

Ad Infinitum

LEATHER SUPPLIERS

This is a partial listing of some of the leather suppliers across the country who might fill orders for leather. I suggest that you write to the one nearest you (perhaps enclosing a self-addressed return envelope) and ask if they will handle small orders for whatever skins you wish to purchase. If not, ask where you can obtain leather in your area.

(List courtesy of the Tanners Council of America)

CALIFORNIA

California Crafts Supply
1419 N. Central Park Ave.
Anaheim, Calif. 92802

Calnap Tanning Co.
101 S. Coombs St.
Napa, Calif. 94558

Legallet Tanning Co.
1099 Quesada Ave.
San Francisco, Calif. 94124

Los Angeles Tanning Co.
4101 Whiteside St.
Los Angeles, Calif. 90063

MacPherson Brothers
P.O. Box 395
San Francisco, Calif. 94101

Manasse-Block Tanning Co.
1300 Fourth St.
Berkeley, Calif. 94710

Metten and Gebhardt Inc.
1775 Egbert Ave.
San Francisco, Calif. 94124

Salz Leathers Inc.
P.O. Box 238
Santa Cruz, Calif. 95060

GEORGIA

Bona Allen
(Division of Tandy Corp.)
P.O. Box 229
Buford, Georgia 30518

ILLINOIS

Acme Sponge and Chamois Co.
2421 N. Division St.
Chicago, Ill. 60622

Griess-Pfleger Tanning Co.
1251 Sand St.
Waukegan, Ill. 60085

A. H. Ross and Sons
1229-35 N. Branch St.
Chicago, Ill. 60622

Weil and Eisendrath Co.
2221 N. Elston Ave.
Chicago, Ill. 60614

INDIANA

August Barth Leather Co.
E. 10th and River
New Albany, Ind. 47150

George Moser Leather Co.
Silver St. and Penn R.R.
New Albany, Ind. 47150

IOWA

Boone Enterprises Inc.
Industrial Park Road
Boone, Iowa 50036

KENTUCKY

Caldwell Lace Leather Co.
1 Caldwell St.
Auburn, Ky. 42206

MAINE

Prime Tanning Co.
Berwick, Me. 03401

Kirstein Leather Co.
72 Main St.
Saco, Me. 04072

Camden Tanning Corp.
116 Washington St.
Camden, Me. 04843

Wilton Tanning Co.
Box 55
East Wilton, Me. 04234

MARYLAND

J. M. Bucheimer Co.
P.O. Box 280
Frederick, Md. 21701

W. D. Byron and Sons Inc.
Williamsport, Md. 21795

MASSACHUSETTS

Allied Kid Co.
209 South St.
Boston, Mass. 02111

Beggs and Cobb Inc.
179 South St.
Boston, Mass. 02111

Philip F. Boynton Inc.
166 Main St.
Peabody, Mass. 01960

Shrut and Asch Leather Co.
83 South St.
Boston, Mass. 02111

Carr Leather Co.
500 Boston St.
Lynn, Mass. 01905

Fermon Leather Co.
27 Walnut St.
Peabody, Mass. 01960

Richard Leather Co.
9 Webb St.
Salem, Mass. 01970

MICHIGAN

Eagle Ottawa Leather Co.
P.O. Box 308
Grand Haven, Mich. 49417

Whitehall Leather Co.
Lake St.
Whitehall, Mich. 49461

Wolverine Worldwide
9341 Courtland Drive
Rockford, Mich. 49341

MINNESOTA

S. B. Foot Trading Co.
P.O. Box 73
Red Wing, Minn. 55066

MISSOURI

Blueside Co.
Spur 759 at Florence Road
St. Joseph, Mo. 64504

Hermann Oak Leather Co.
4050 N. First St.
St. Louis, Mo. 63147

Rey Manufacturing Corp.
P.O. Box 340
Cape Girardeau, Mo. 63701

NEW HAMPSHIRE

E. Cummings Leather Co.
High St.
Lebanon, N.H. 03766

Greene Tanning Corp.
Water St.
Milton Mills, N.H. 03852

Granite State Leathers
Fairmont St.
Nashua, N.H. 03060

Seal Tanning Co.
Commercial St.
Manchester, N.H. 03101

United Tanners Inc.
9 Orchard St.
Dover, N.H. 03820

NEW JERSEY

Barrett and Co.
49 Vesey St.
Newark, N.J. 07105

Globe Tanning Corp.
681 Main St.
Belleville, N.J. 07109

Goldsmith Leather Co.
50 Paris St.
Newark, N.J. 07105

H. Schwarz Leather Co.
Garden Place and River Road
Edgewater, N.J. 07020

Southern Trading Corp.
442 Frelinghuysen Ave.
Newark, N.J. 07114

NEW YORK

Amour Leather Co.
525 Broadway
New York City 10012

Cromwell Leather Co.
45 West 34 St.
New York City 10001

Eastmor Leather Trading Co.
83 Bleecker St.
Gloversville, N.Y. 12078

Hochhauser Leather Co.
171 Madison Ave.
New York City 10016

Karg Brothers Inc.
6–20 E. Fulton St.
Johnstown, N.Y. 12095

Paul N. Stern Leather Co.
16 West 19 St.
New York City 10011

NORTH CAROLINA

Drutan Products Inc.
P.O. Box 1140
Goldsboro, N.C. 27530

OHIO

Sidney Tanning Co.
218 N. Ohio Ave.
Sidney, Ohio 45365

Ohio Leather Co.
1052 N. State St.
Girard, Ohio 44420

Conneaut Leather Co.
W. Adams St.
Conneaut, Ohio 44030

OREGON

Frontier Leather Co.
1210 E. Pacific St.
P.O. Box 502
Sherwood, Ore. 97140

Muir and McDonald Co.
100 Levens St.
Dallas, Ore. 97338

PENNSYLVANIA

William Amer Co.
215 Willow St.
Philadelphia, Pa. 19123

Eberle Tanning Co.
360 Church St.
Westfield, Pa. 16950

McAdoo and Allen Welting Co.
Quakertown
(Bucks County), Pa. 18951

RHODE ISLAND

Whitehall Leather Co.
55 Dupont Drive
Providence, R.I. 02907

TENNESSEE

Coey Tanning Co.
Wartrace, Tenn. 37183

Genesco Inc.
Genesco Park, Route F-240
Nashville, Tenn. 37202

Scholze Tannery
3100 St. Elmo Ave.
Chattanooga, Tenn. 37408

Tennessee Tanning Co.
915 N. Atlantic St.
Tullahoma, Tenn. 37388

VIRGINIA

American Lace Leather Co.
P.O. Box 121
Richmond, Va. 23225

WISCONSIN

Berlin Tanning Co.
235 S. Wisconsin
Berlin, Wis. 54423

Blackhawk Tanners Inc.
1000 W. Bruce St.
Milwaukee, Wis. 53204

General Split Corp.
5050 S. 2nd St.
Milwaukee, Wis. 53207

Midwest Tanning Co.
1200 Davis Ave.
S. Milwaukee, Wis. 53172

INDEX